smartlittleowl.com

ACTIVITY BOOK
FOR 3-4 YEAR OLDS

D1397106

THIS BOOK BELONGS TO:

- -

- -

Receive a FREE gift!

Go to our website and download for free the printable tracing book.

smartlittleowl.com/gift

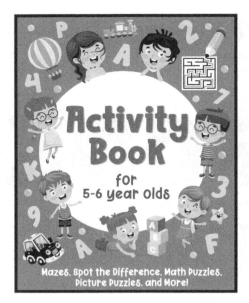

Activity Book for 5-6 year olds

Mazes, Spot the Difference, Math Puzzles, Picture Puzzles, and More!

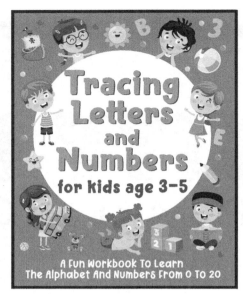

Tracing Letters and Numbers for kids age 3-5

A Fun Workbook To Learn The Alphabet And Numbers From 0 TO 20

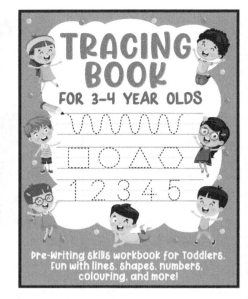

TRACING BOOK FOR 3-4 YEAR OLDS

Pre-Writing skills workbook for Toddlers. Fun with lines, shapes, numbers, colouring, and more!

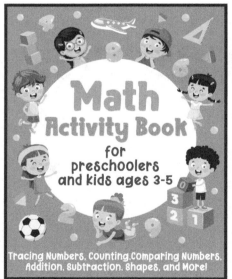

Math Activity Book for preschoolers and kids ages 3-5

Tracing Numbers, Counting, Comparing Numbers, Addition, Subtraction, Shapes, and More!

YES, I SPY! I SPY ... ANIMALS

YES, I SPY! I SPY ... EVERYTHING

SEE MORE OF OUR PRODUCTS

 amazon

Books ▾ | smart little owl |

Trace the lines.

Letter **A**

Colour the letters.

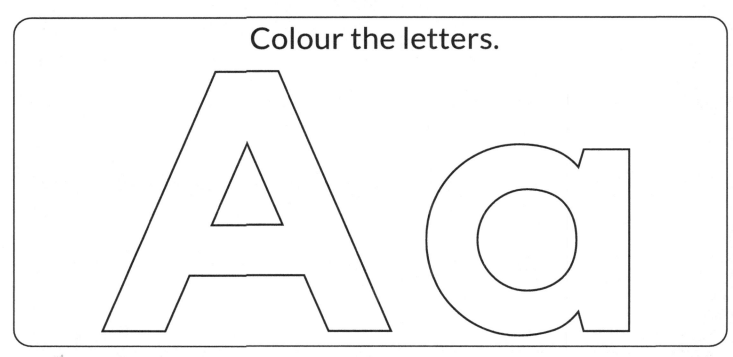

Colour the pictures that start with the letter A.

Find 3 differences, then colour the images.

Find the right path.

Letter **B**

Colour the letters.

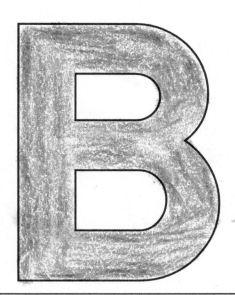 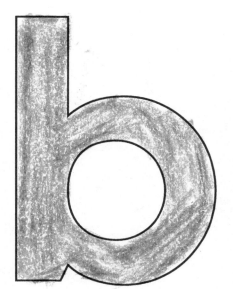

Colour the pictures that start with the letter B.

Trace and colour the flower.

Match the animals to their homes.

Letter **C**

Colour the letters.

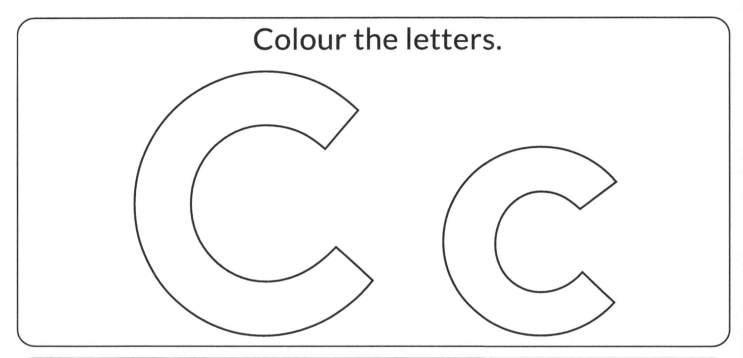

Colour the pictures that start with the letter C.

Count the fingers and thumbs on the hands.
Trace the numbers.

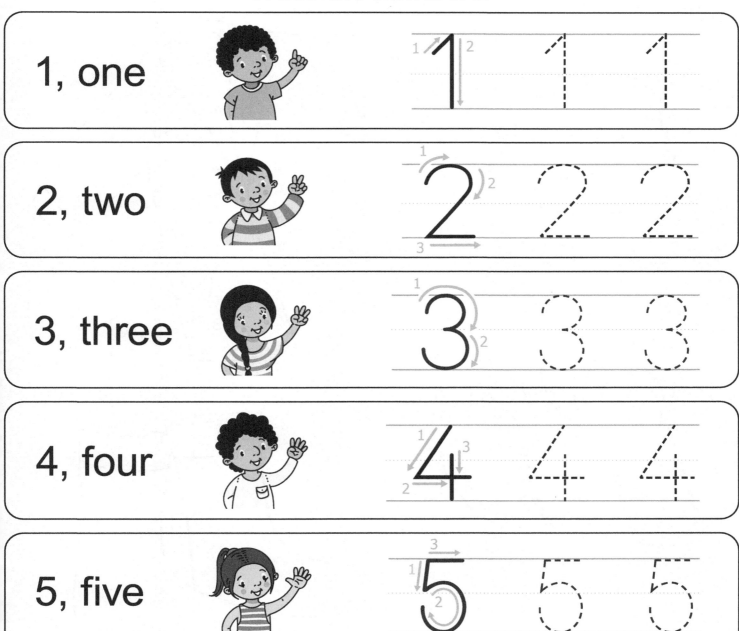

1, one

2, two

3, three

4, four

5, five

Colour the clothes you wear when it rains.

Letter **D**

Colour the letters.

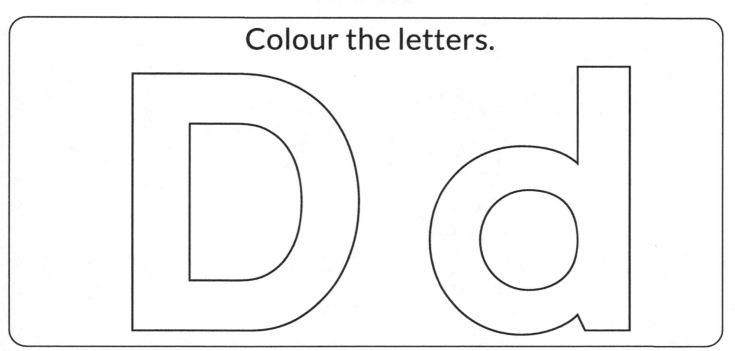

Colour the pictures that start with the letter D.

Trace the lines.

Circle the object that is heavier.

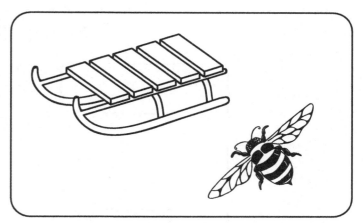

Letter **E**

Colour the letters.

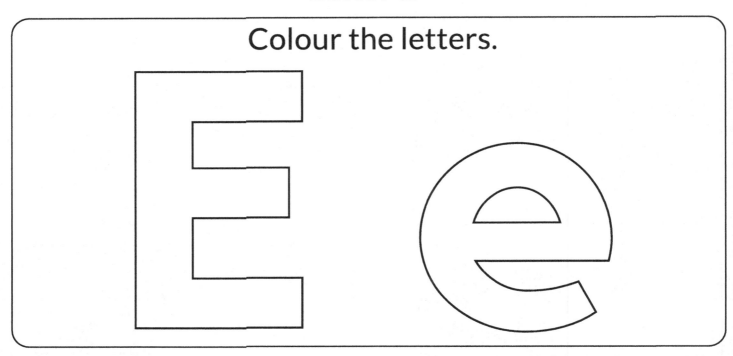

Colour the pictures that start with the letter E.

Count and write how many.

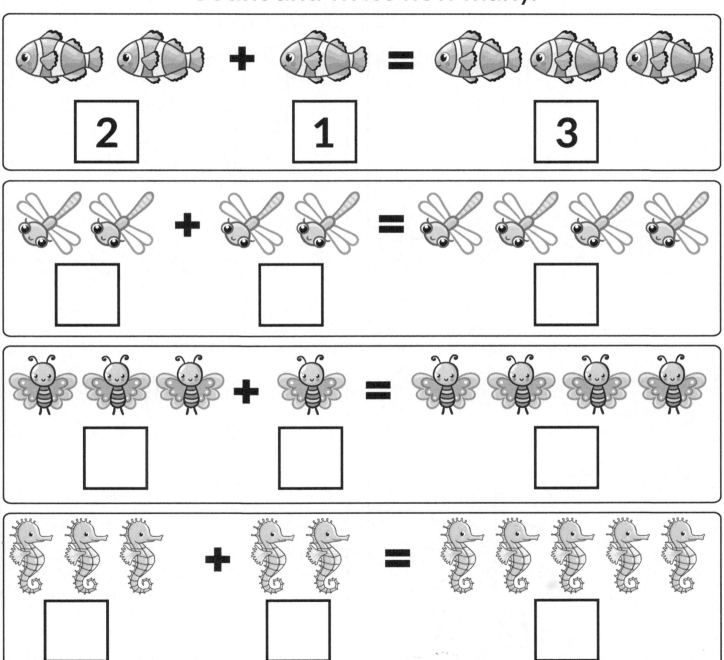

Colour the two pictures in each box that rhyme.

Letter **F**

Colour the letters.

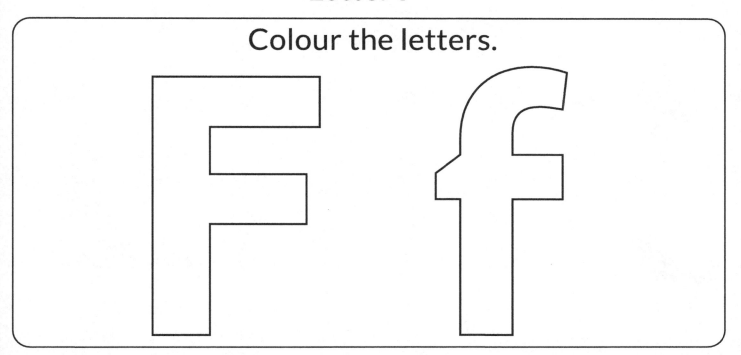

Colour the pictures that start with the letter F.

Draw a line to connect each picture with its other half.

Circle the picture that is different than the rest.

Letter **G**

Colour the letters.

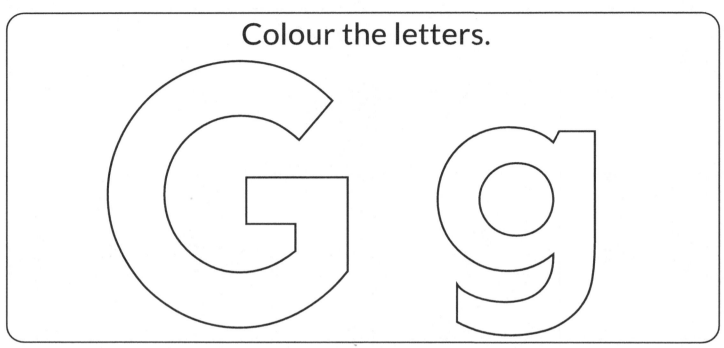

Colour the pictures that start with the letter G.

Colour the vegetables.

Draw the lines matching each picture to its shadow.

Letter **H**

Colour the letters.

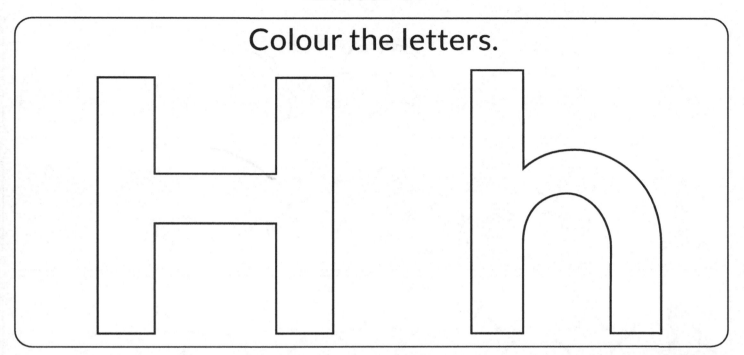

Colour the pictures that start with the letter H.

Count and colour the correct number.

Tick (✔) the taller animal.

Tick (✔) the shorter animal.

Letter I

Colour the letters.

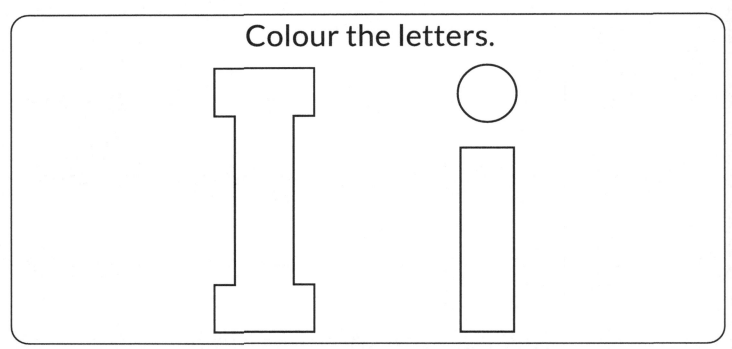

Colour the pictures that start with the letter I.

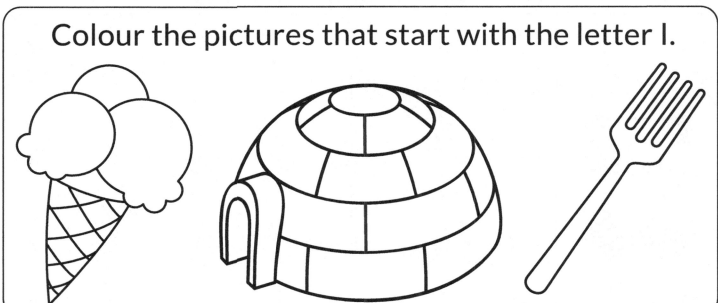

Colour the shape in each box that is the smallest.

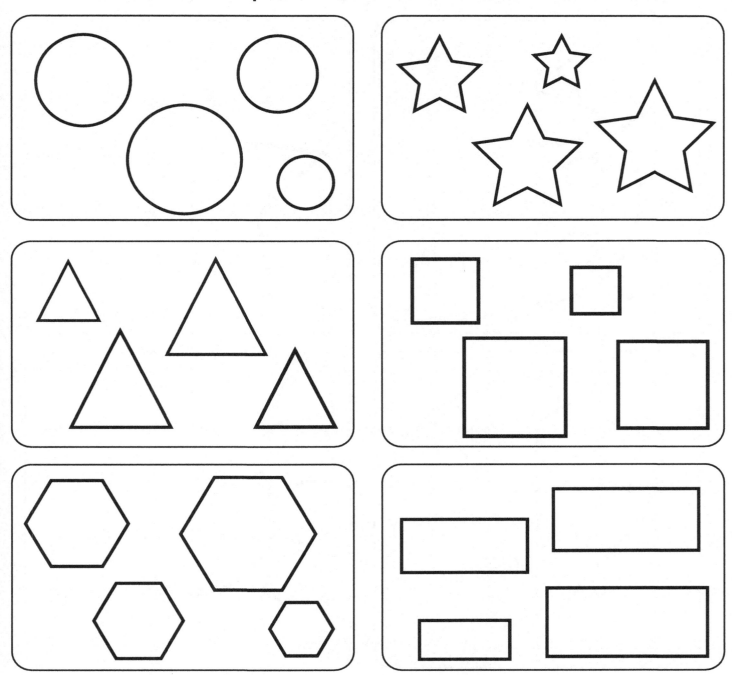

Complete the other half of each picture.

Letter **J**

Colour the letters.

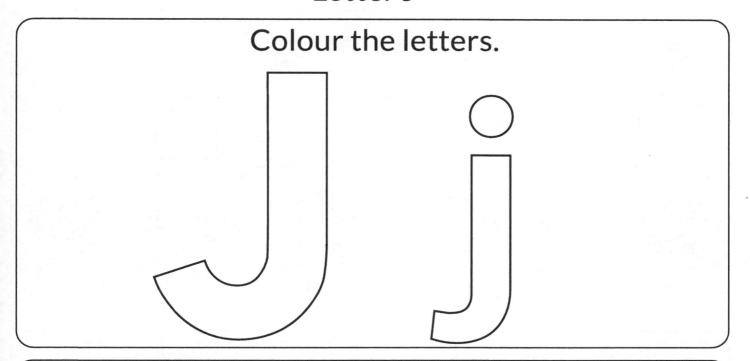

Colour the pictures that start with the letter J.

Count and write how many.

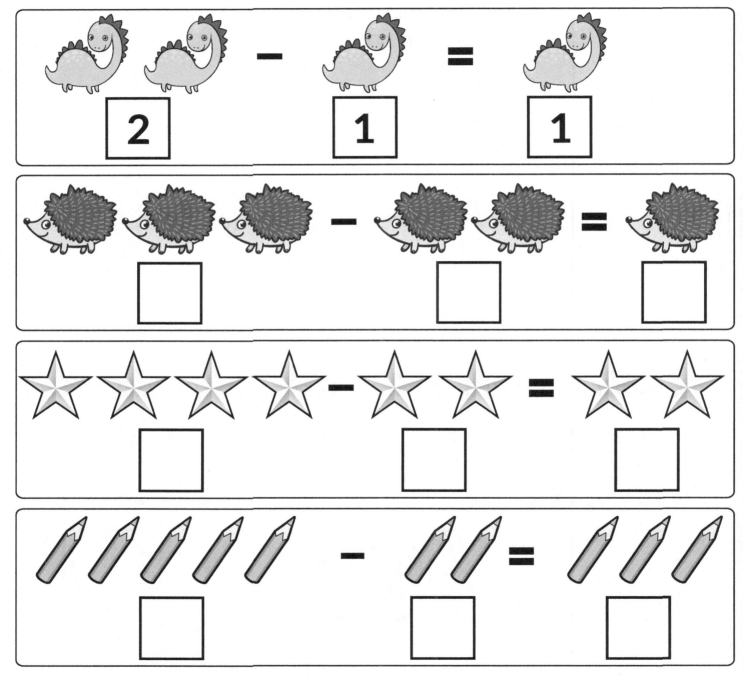

Colour the biggest car.

Letter K

Colour the letters.

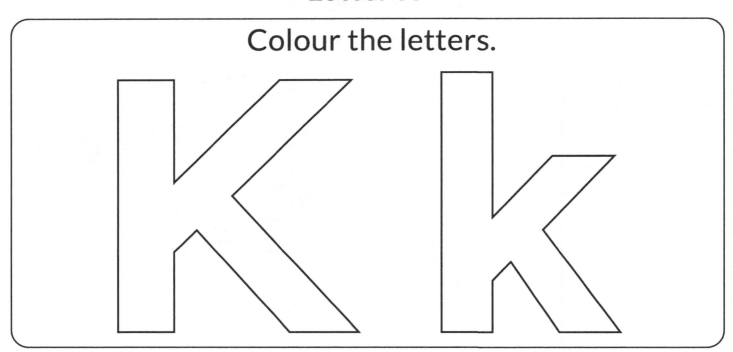

Colour the pictures that start with the letter K.

Dinosaur Colouring Page.

Find 3 differences, then colour the images.

Letter **L**

Colour the letters.

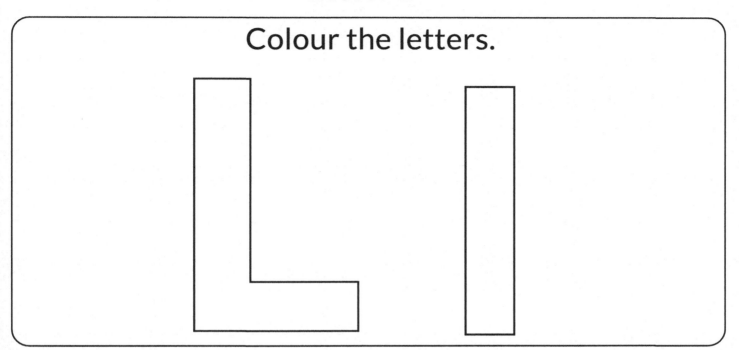

Colour the pictures that start with the letter L.

Trace the shapes.

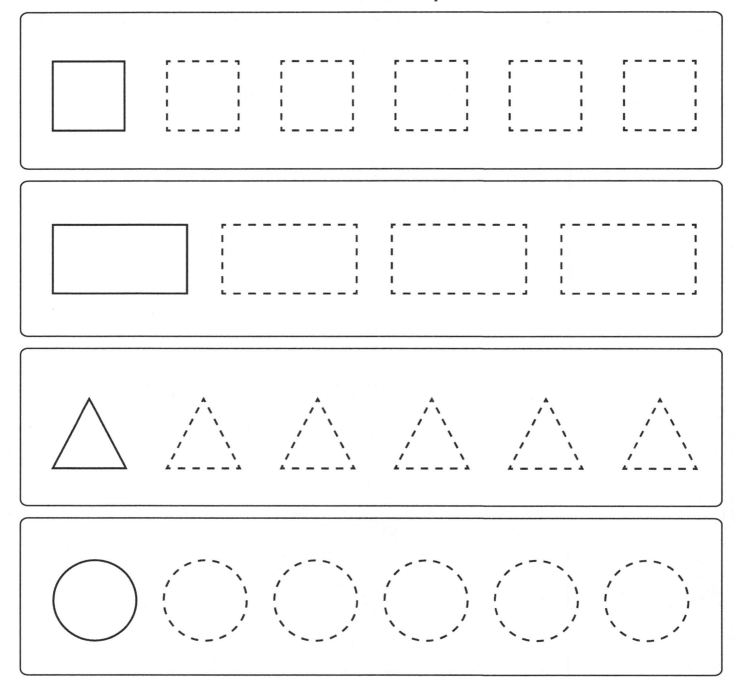

Colour by number 1 -5.

1 - blue   2 - red   3 - black   4 - orange   5- gray

Letter **M**

Colour the letters.

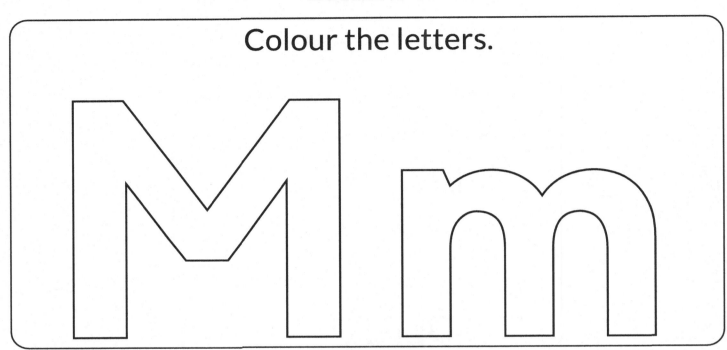

Colour the pictures that start with the letter M.

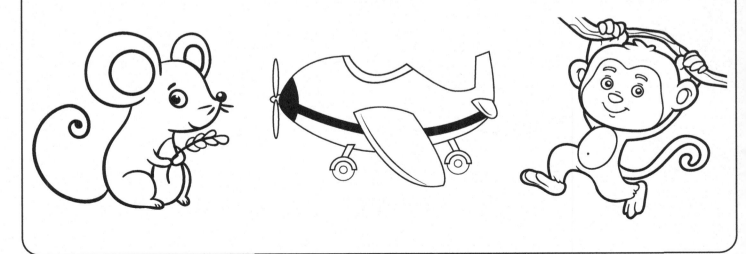

Connect the same ones.

Complete the pattern.

Letter **N**

Colour the letters.

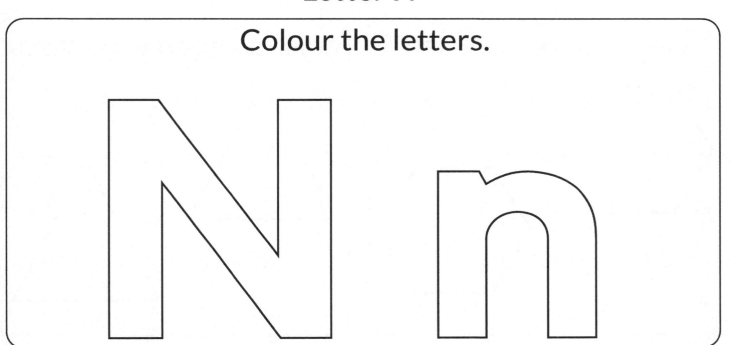

Colour the pictures that start with the letter N.

Left and right position.

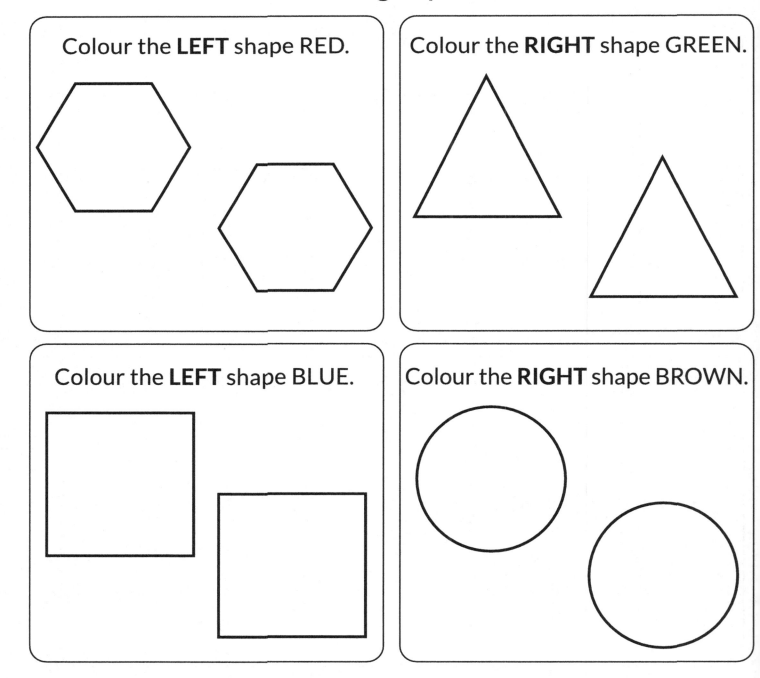

Colour the **LEFT** shape RED.

Colour the **RIGHT** shape GREEN.

Colour the **LEFT** shape BLUE.

Colour the **RIGHT** shape BROWN.

Trace the lines.

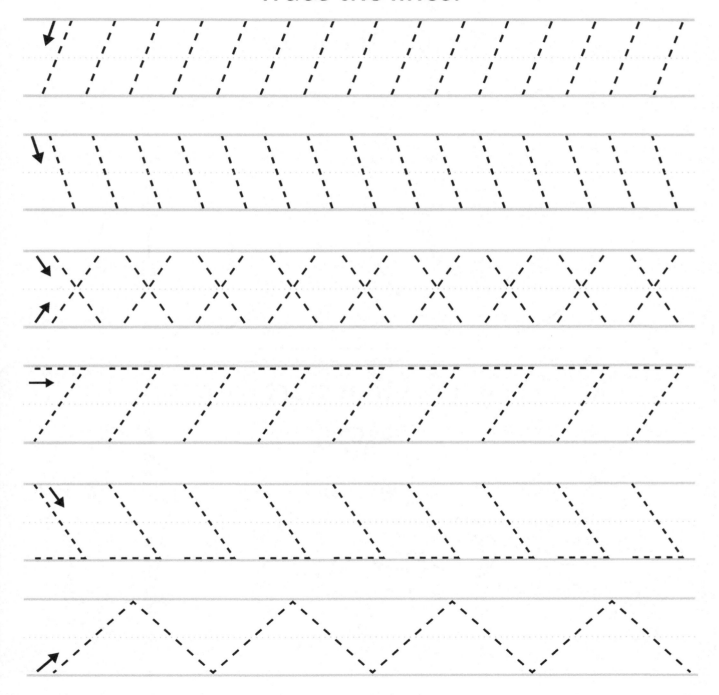

Letter O

Colour the letters.

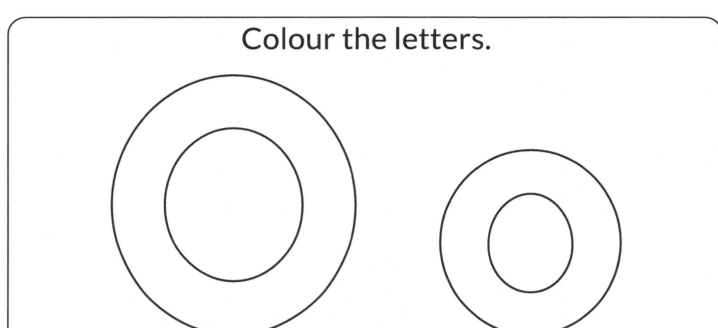

Colour the pictures that start with the letter O.

Look at the animals in each box,
and colour the group that has more.

Colour by dots.

· black · : yellow · : red · :: green · :: brown

Letter **P**

Colour the letters.

Colour the pictures that start with the letter P.

Colour the things you can eat.

Find 3 differences, then colour the images.

Letter **Q**

Colour the letters.

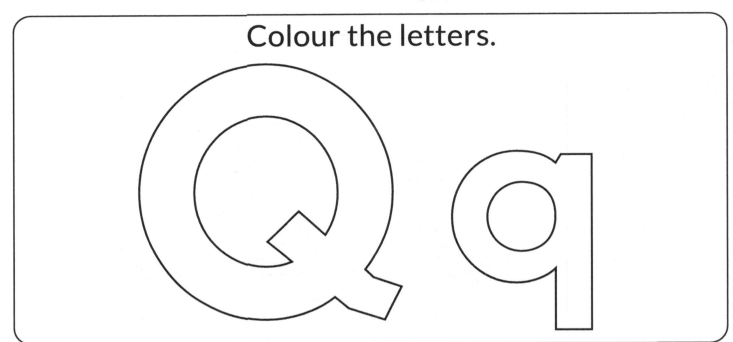

Colour the pictures that start with the letter Q.

Draw the lines matching each picture to its shadow.

Trace the lines.

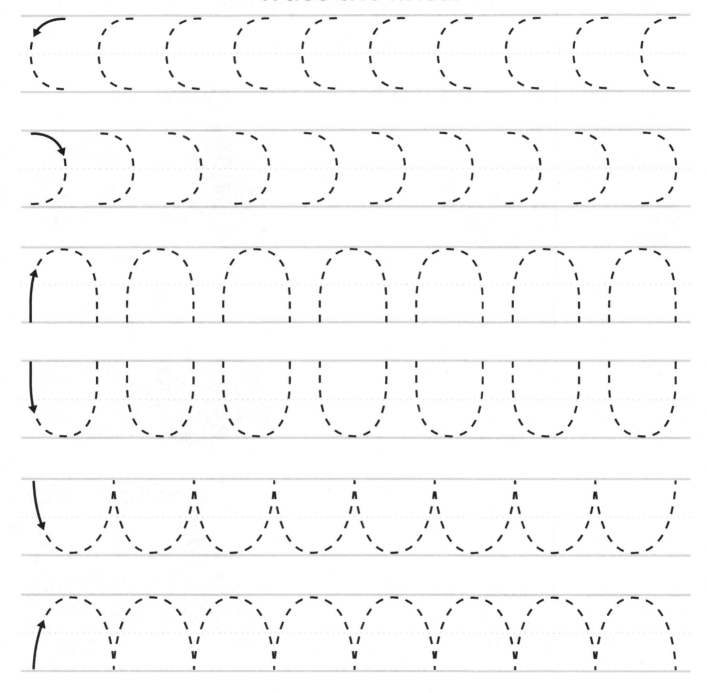

Letter **R**

Colour the letters.

Colour the pictures that start with the letter R.

Find the right path.

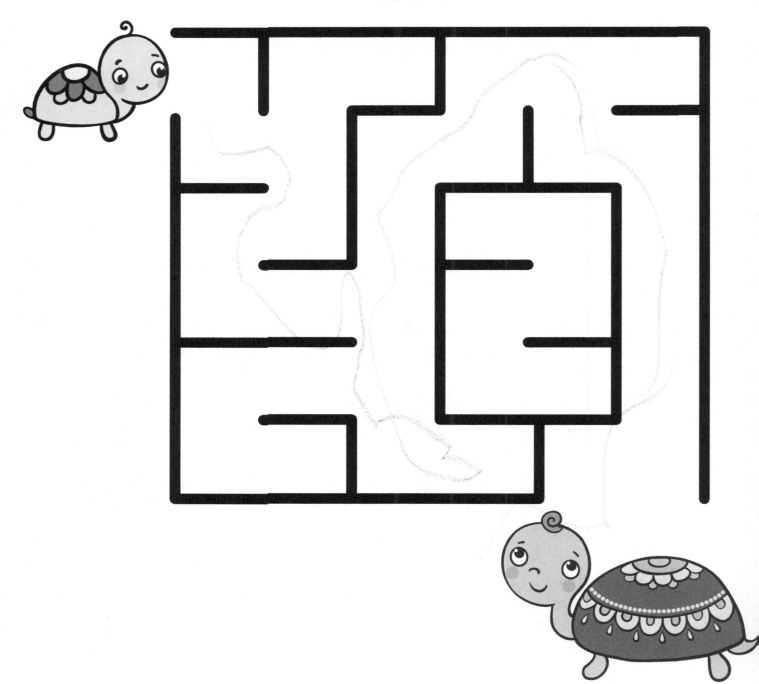

Trace and colour the dolphin.

Letter **S**

Colour the letters.

Colour the pictures that start with the letter S.

Count and write how many.

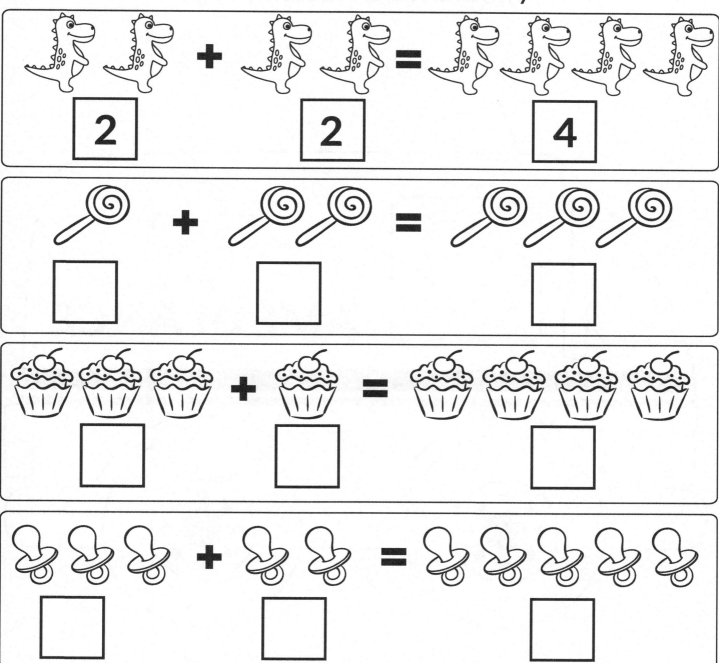

2 + 2 = 4

Ambulance Colouring Page.

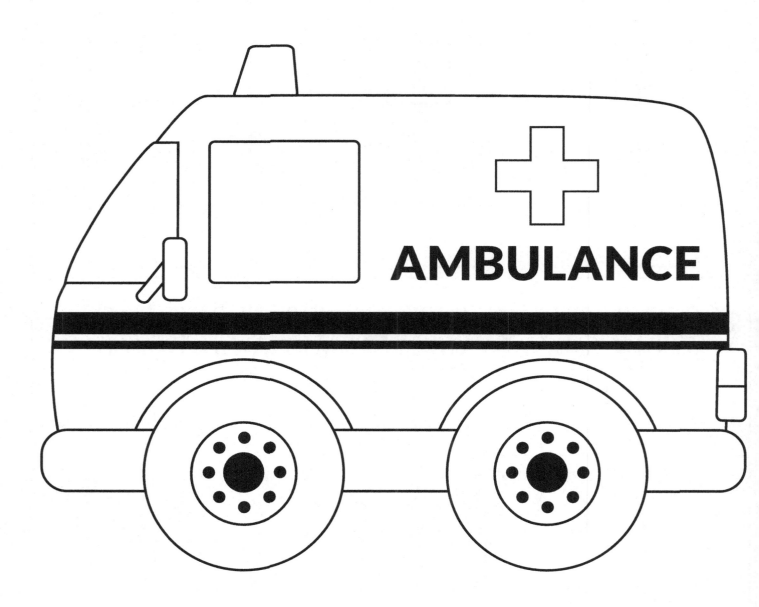

Letter T

Colour the letters.

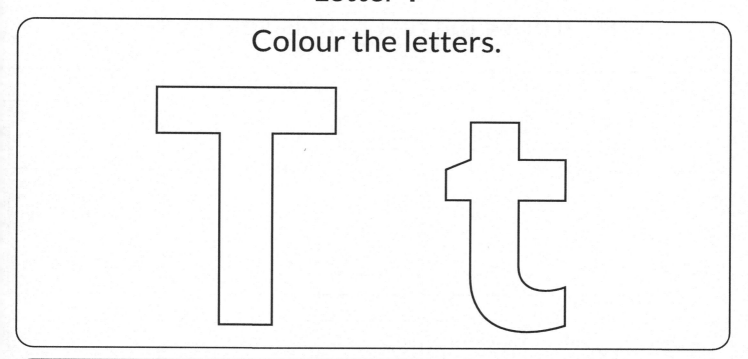

Colour the pictures that start with the letter T.

Look at the order of the shapes.
Then draw the rest to finish each row.

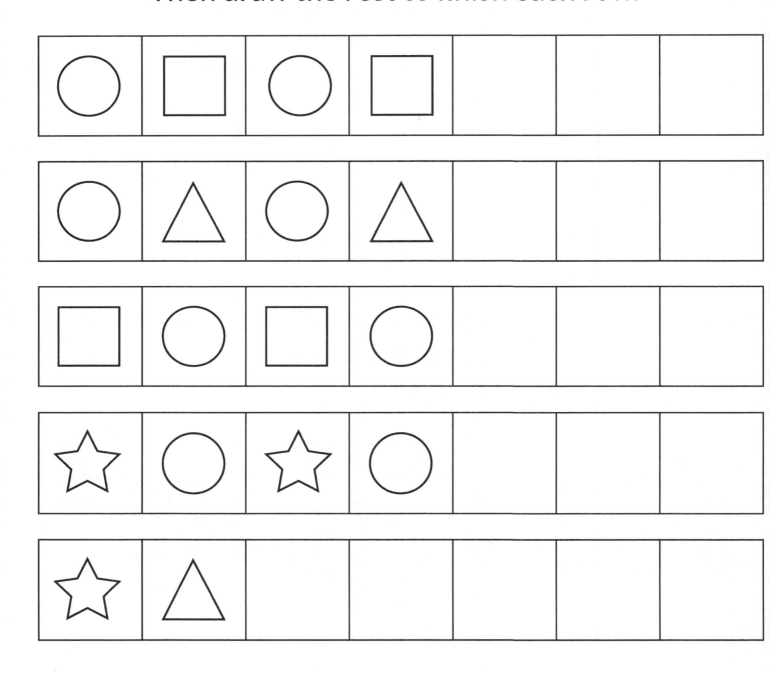

Circle the biggest picture in each row.

Letter **U**

Colour the letters.

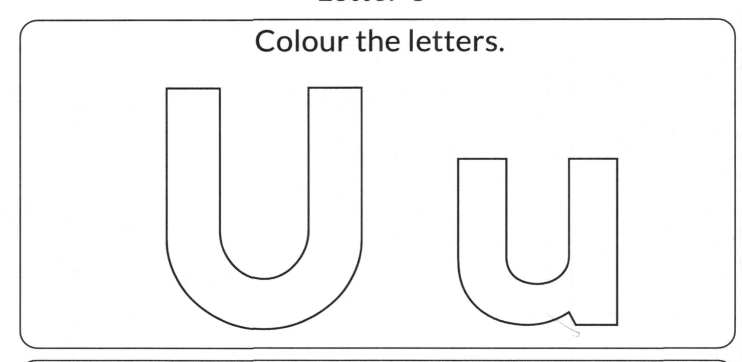

Colour the pictures that start with the letter U.

Find and colour all triangles.

Find the right path.

Letter **V**

Colour the letters.

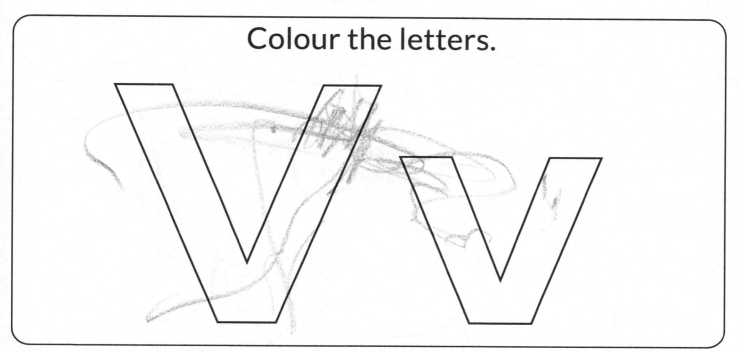

Colour the pictures that start with the letter V.

Elephant Colouring Page.

Circle the picture that is different than the rest.

Letter **W**

Colour the letters.

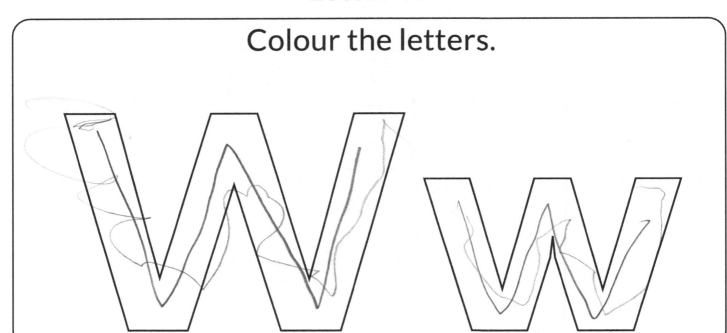

Colour the pictures that start with the letter W.

whale

wolf

Colour the SOFT objects.

Trace the lines.

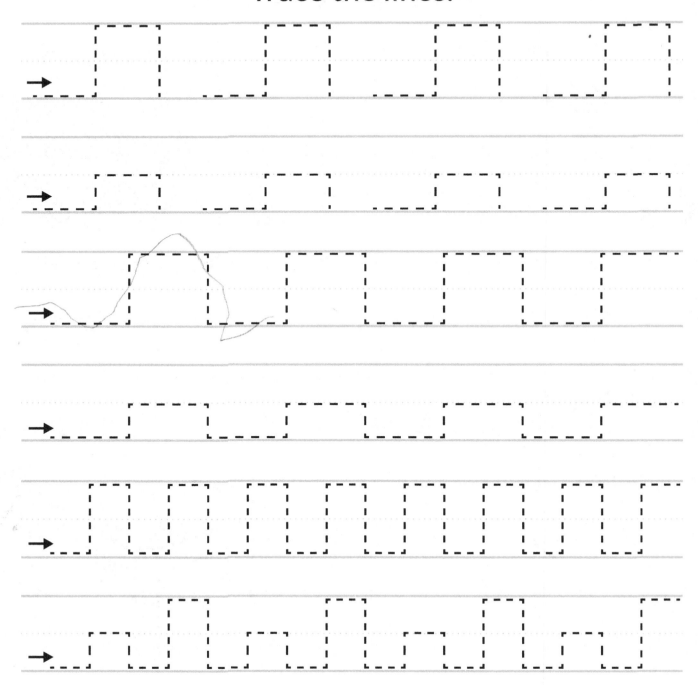

Letter **X**

Colour the letters.

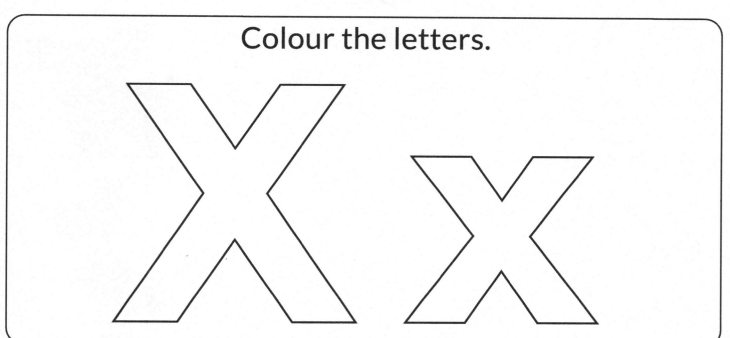

Colour the picture that start with the letter X.

Draw the lines matching each picture to its shadow.

Complete the pattern.

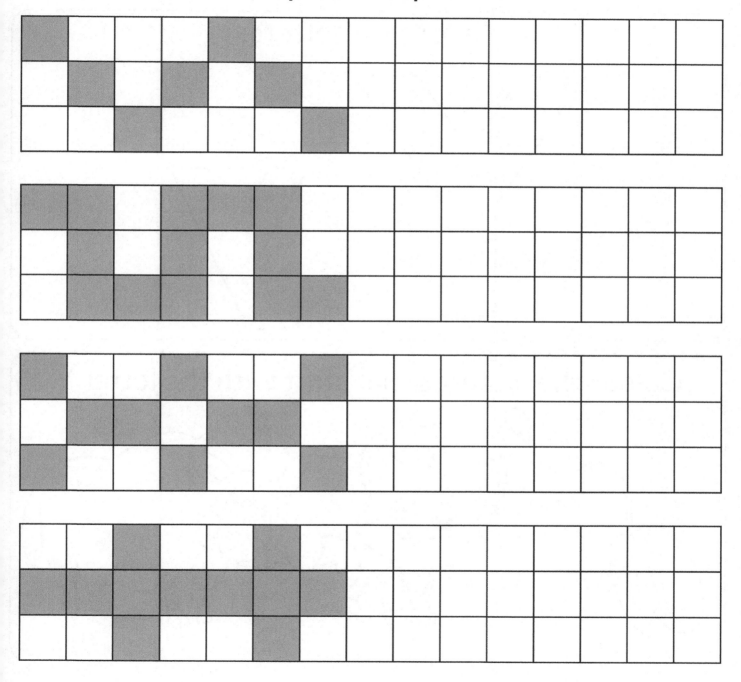

Letter Y

Colour the letters.

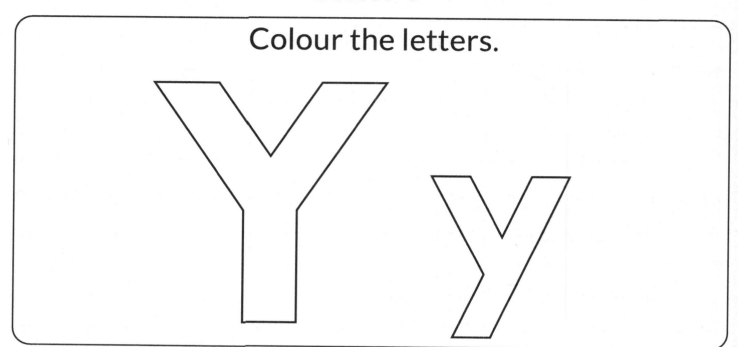

Colour the pictures that start with the letter Y.

Locomotive Colouring Page.

Find the right path.

Letter **Z**

Colour the letters.

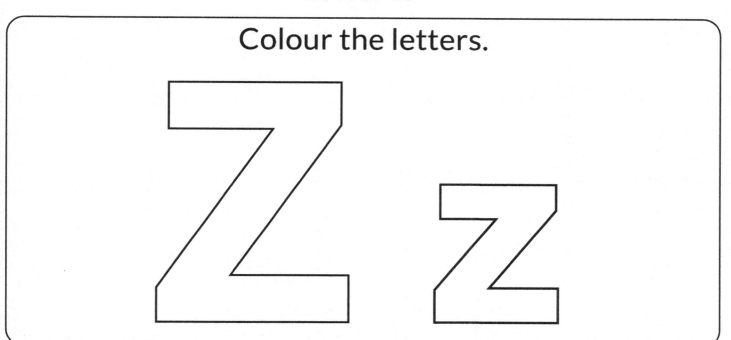

Colour the pictures that start with the letter Z.

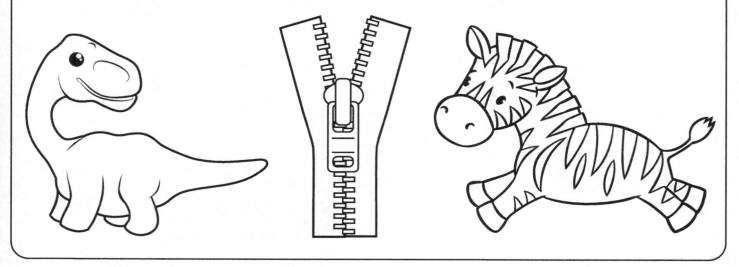

Made in United States
North Haven, CT
16 February 2023